the white calf kicks

the
white calf
kicks

poems by DEBORAH SLICER

*Autumn House
Press*

© 2003 Deborah Slicer

"Autumn House" and "Autumn House Press" are registered trademarks owned by Autumn House Press, a non-profit corporation whose mission is the publication and promotion of poetry.

Text and cover design: Kathy Boykowycz
Editorial Consultant: Eva Maria Simms
Marketing Consultant: Michael Wurster
Cover Photograph: "Wheatfield, Western Montana" by Tim Cooper
Author photograph: Lynn Sainsbury

Printed in the USA
ISBN: 0966941969
Library of Congress Control Number: 2003110471

*For the "Tree Farm," Elk Mountain,
Pennsylvania; the Virginia Blue Ridge;
Montana, east and west.*

*And for my mother,
Vilma Grace Slicer (1927-1965)*

Contents

The Autumn House Poetry Series
Michael Simms, editor

OneOnOne by Jack Myers
Snow White Horses, Selected Poems 1973-1988 by Ed Ochester
The Leaving, New and Selected Poems by Sue Ellen Thompson
Dirt by Jo McDougall
Fire in the Orchard by Gary Margolis
Just Once, New and Previous Poems by Samuel Hazo
The White Calf Kicks by Deborah Slicer
   (2003 Autumn House Poetry Prize, selected by Naomi Shihab Nye)
The Divine Salt by Peter Blair
The Dark Takes Aim by Julie Suk

Acknowledgments

Virginia Quarterly Review, "Loco," "Sunflowers, Wyoming," "O Merciful God (and Some Angels)"
Green Mountains Review, "Highline Cosmology, Montana"
Tar River, "Snow," "Outside Richmond, Virginia, Sunday"
Cutbank, "Thinking of Kierkegaard"
Poetry Northwest, "Pastoral"
Southern Poetry Review, "Dissonate Psalm in Late Summer"

Many thanks to the following cast of dear characters for their invaluable contributions to this manuscript: Bridget Clarke, Christa Countryman, Rita Dove, Chris Dombrowski, Jim Baker Hall, Bev Jackson, Thorpe Moeckel, Naomi Shihab Nye, Greg Orr, Beth Parker, Michael and Eva Simms, Jami Sindelar, Kyle Thompson, Charles Wright, my colleagues in the philosophy department at the University of Montana, the creative writing program at the University of Virginia, and T.C.

All royalties for this book will be donated to the National Forest Protection Alliance and to Women's Voices for the Earth.

Flare up like flame
and make big shadows I can move in.

Let everything happen to you: beauty and terror.
Just keep going. No feeling is final.
Don't let yourself lose me.

"God speaks to each of us as he makes us"
—Rilke

Loco

If titmouse wags her song at me again like a scolding finger—*you-loco*—
    I aim to pop her,
then lie down among the cows and rusting tractors along the creekside,
    frigid,
while the bull soliloquizes like widower Macbeth.
    For the milk of human kindness doth flow from mine ears
and I have murderous thoughts
    against myself
because I didn't grieve you better.

If that same murder of crows bobs the back field in their blackcoats
    like a convention of metaphysicians
muttering *Kant-kant-kant-kant,*
    I'll give them one barrel of heaven, the other hell.
My buck fawn's back legs yodel through the early morning plenary,
    my buck fawn runs their arguments reductio
loco. His tongue shinnies up their one-eyed sunflower stalks,
    his back talk pins their heavy-headed arguments to the ground.
Come winter I'll eat my own hands before those oily axioms touch my mouth.

If bobwhite calls her lover's name in her sleep at dusk,
    reminding me, again, I'm loverless, lonesome
as a criminal past, well, then—
    what? Make another meal of self-pity?
Oh World, blow your noise through the keyhole of me,
    so when Night walks by on its tip-toes with its ear to the wall of my bedroom
let it hear the loco-commotion
    of the bus stop at five-fifteen on any Friday afternoon.

I have a crazy angel in my throat.
      She grabs sorrow by the ankles, swings it round,
round in my mouth,
      until it's a tale of childish fury,
signifying the best it can—
      a fluster of wings in the chimney, ashes sassing.
Blood bird,
      my bird, she eats the ashes;

these ashes are enough.

Snow

1

On Main Street
in a small town
in southern Indiana,
Jimmy's has a sign out front
advertising custom cuts of meat.
At night, the only lights in town
are the two flashing traffic lights
and the yellow light
inside the small holding pen.
Where the cows are packed so tight,
they cannot move backward
nor forward,
not yet.
They must stand there,
as still,
as expectant
as the hour just before snow.

2

At five in the morning
on a side street
near the breweries
in downtown Cincinnati,
a man steps out of the building to light a cigarette.
There's ice on the stoop,
and the wind is pushing snow in his face.
A few blocks south in the city,
ice on the river is sounding open,
Kentucky and Ohio
breaking a bone between them.
At this hour there is nothing else.
Only the soft cusps of snow striking his apron
and the blood there
reasserting itself.
The beginning of an argument.

Having It Out with Life over Breakfast

Wet snow batters the winter plains like catfish fillets,
as sleet skids
across the tin roof,
popping.
My blue Dodge by the barn burrows under snow's soft blouse to suck.

World—
World—why am I so
hungry?

Make your biscuits like you used to—with the grape jelly grimace,
eggs over easy. Tabasco
so they squawk.
Boil coffee till it grunts, *Honey...*
come 'ere, spoon-feed it
bourbon, brown sugar.
Set the orange on its white plate where it beats its chest laughing
at us.

I've watched the sun dress this row of winter trees
in the same gray tweeds
morning after morning,
a pocketful of vireos sings like spare change, and I begin to
hope. But
you ladle up the same flood of loose grits, disembowel
the little orange with a kitchen knife, leaving
rind on my fork,
where it smells of every grievance since the very beginning.

Listen, You—

I am dog-paddling
through a kettle of Quaker's
cooked oats
just to think this, climbing
up a sweaty glass of last night's beer
to say it loud enough:

We were once equal
parts cream to
sugar and the cause
of many electrical fires in the kitchen.

Now the sum of all your verbs is lighter than a snowflake.
Drifts gagging the one road out.

Highline Cosmology, Montana
[Janet, age 8]

I hear the creek bobtail down its highway tonight
toward the Milk.
And the cold Canada wind jake-
                              brakes
for all the little cottonwoods
wantin' which way to Wolf Point, Rabbit, Yaak.
I hate being the one always left behind!

Some nights I climb up on this house just to yell:

Burrrr-llinggg-tonnn—

                    —Norrrrr-therrrrrn

like the freight trains up Havre,
                    else nobody else remembers
we're alive. Fact is
                    I'm missing someone,
                                        someones.

Fact is
          people I love
                    die. And I want them back.

Where have you put them?

Are my brothers in your white caves in the White Cliffs
          along your Missouri,
                              laid cold as caught fish?
Where's Pika my Pinto
                    who rolled down the Knees
          of God,
                    and why
didn't you help her?

Last year my father took a truck belly full of Herefords across the Divide
where everything, even the wind, blows backwards,
          and now he's got lost. My mother says
nothing belongs to us
               forever, even the spark
for the firebox is on loan.
                 And I hate you for that.

I think we are born wild horses
with a catch rope attached to you.
      I will

drag your punk butt
down the Porcupine
River from Pop-Top
to Peck,
and your hollering—

         Ouch-Ouch-Ouch-

OUCH!—will just be spurs
in my wild stallion's sides. Then,

I'll give your fool's face a good taste of every rip-rock up on Rocky Boy, till
your mind's bashed to bits

              like what's left
            of a Christmas peppermint stick,

till your backbone twists
            like the world's longest licorice whip,

till your heart's a-tomic,
a fireball so bad even your own mother can't handle it,

                                       so you'll know what it feels like

            to be me,

so you'll remember
          and remember it good—

you don't own me.

                ▼

I want my dead back.

One springtime my father trucked cattle for slaughter up Sunburst
and rode home with a fat wallet

                       and me in his lap.
But later when we opened the truck ramp to clean up the slap

            we could not believe
our old bull Travis come trottin' out the back
                         into a

      HALLELUJAH

             of buttercups.

Release them like that.

Cancer: Two Lyrics
—L.& I.

1. *Uterus*

Hail
falls through the cosmic cracks
at three in the afternoon
spaaps
at the windows, *pffssts*
at the sun, all the grape hyacinths
break down.

(a-nurse-calls-says-you-fell-through-the-cracks-last-year. so. sorry.)

You said—?

Fucking

      Not

      Funny.

One: Refuse

the air's conspiracies. Bite

the light. Two:

      Gut-

       punch
drops of rain. Three: Kick

         brains out of dirt.

Four: If
     wind shoves

             shove   back. Five:

Six: Scratch

the buff peach. When. Seven: it rocks   Eight: like a man's
   ass

     in your hand. Nine: Jack—Nine:

boot
   the twin
       plums. Nine: In their skin—

             sack. Nine:

Because.
     If.

    Nine: God: Nine: If: Nine: Exists: God: Nine:
          Deserves—
               (Fucking—
                  Fucking not funny!)
                     This!

Wet snow now,
heavy as bathtubs–

Oh knock us unconscious!

2. After Your Mastectomy

Sun reached inside my black sweater today
fumbling all around in there, hurried and

hot. And I remembered you telling me about the first boy

who made you laugh
during sex,

when he'd take your brown nipple
inside his mouth,

                      suck

sigh—

horehound   *horehound*

Lucky boy.

Sunflowers, Wyoming

Wednesday, west of Sheridan, sky
flattens out like a dinner plate,

                      distance

runs a marathon into Montana,
never gets winded, never turns for a backward glance at the Big Horns,

wind
                undresses the unleavened west two hundred miles to Stillwater.

Joy-running, a red balloon crisscrosses the highway in front of my truck.

Then caught in forty-mile-an-hour gusts it turns panicked
circles, seeking
some tether, clutch
of creekside willow, chokecherry,
bitterbrush.

      Have I been this reckless with my life?
During all those years I walked with my hands behind my back
     did I strangle every opportunity
for love, pick-pocket pity on street corners, pray
     to a beautiful but indifferent grievance,
waiting for a rose thorn to bloom?

Yesterday, east of Sheridan,
fields of September sunflowers hung their collared heads, multitudes
at the Vatican, miles
of humility.
        Drove faster.

Mousey and Me

If you think like a Holstein
who's stood cramped in a grey stall

all six months of winter, waiting
for the first buttercups to push up snow in the pasture

like clabber rising through milk,
then you know the penalty

for swatting the bony man in thick glasses
with a piss-soaked tail

that stings like fire thrown in his face:
You get a beating with

whatever's handy—the bucket, a filthy rope,
his fists—on your rump

and maybe all over the head.
Sometimes, when the pain is unbearable

his brothers will have to stop him, throw him into a snowbank,
with his pride.

(Why do you do it, anyway?
                                        Who knows...
He's such an easy target.)

When he leans his strawberry blonde head against you
as he's milking,

mumbling all his heartache
into your belly, usually

the extra weight there's all right.
But when it gets meaner,

when he threatens to move into Floweree and
get rid a all a ya !

then it's not so easy to stand there, take it, or
the strap.

His freckled hands are a fact of life,
and at least they're efficient. Now and then

there's sugar in those fists
that he makes you work a little for—

haul a wagon of muck from the barn
after he's grappled an hour just to teach you the harness,

maybe lower your head down
like you're grateful, demure,

act interested in the neighbor's prize bull, even though he's certifiably
stupid.

That man?
Mousey and me knew him about the same.

The Two Horses

When it was respectably cool that evening
they led the two horses
from the flush field
to the bare yard by the barn.

She tied the mare to the fence,
looped her grey tail into knots, hobbled
her, till she fought like a rocking horse,
back and front.

He led the stallion beside her, as the bay leaned
his huge body toward
a right angle against
the rope.

I'd come for the wild roses
where they jumped the fence in that crook in the road. I'd come for
the sweetness they gave me
when I covered their faces with mine.

The stallion reared up behind her
as she said something
to him, only

one flared syllable
in their own language.
The fence creaked.

And the roses,
I thought they leaned away from me.

Then he came down.
And they praised the pair in belling voices
meant for obedient children.

Then each rose in the valley
it turned its face from me
as I walked back alone in the dark.

Geronimo, Running

Shame, you set loose your mumbly little animal
     and it shimmies up my nerve stalk,
enters the stonehouse of my head through the trap door,
     sweet-talks locks to every room instead of knocking.

Inside, ladderback chairs go down on their knees, plead—
     Mercy!
Fists inside the piano pound time
     down to a whine.
Lamplight in the corner finally puts itself out
     of its misery.

By then the last molecules of me are hiding
     in the arroyos of my western hemisphere.
By then I am the starving seven bands following Geronimo
     off San Carlos,
leading the white eyes in one hundred different directions
     for the Madre.

Then I become Geronimo, Geronimo running:
     I run seventy miles on the salt flats the first day, on the second day
I ride my sideways galloping horse,
     by the third,
my horse rides
     me. I call—

Come down, Mother, to anger
     hiding in the Chihuahuas, I call—
Stand up, Father,
     to fear, dog-paddling up the Yaqui.

I give them the single swallow of water I've carried in my mouth
    all day, running,
I give them piñon seeds I've wedged between my back teeth
    all day, hungry,
and still
    they are not satisfied.

They were born old men
    who beat the pots and sing
their death songs
    even when life is long and fat in the mountains.
Their blood is black and yellow.
    Bones in their graves make war with each other for three hundred generations.

Mumbly, my mumbly
    you molt in the face when I look at you.
Spokes burst your wagon wheels when I sing for you.
    You tie yourself up in corn hide, hang
from the willow when I say,
    I love you.

I love you. To finally hold you, mumbly,
    is like one green lake resting on top of the other;
a gentle red fox
    swimming
lifts her tail up out of calm water.

A Few Words about Myself, My Dear Mayakovsky

Sir,
My joie de vivre lies under an enormous fur.
Today, tomorrow, yesterday–
When will the snows melt?

My Thundercloud in Trousers,
Spring pansies are the faces of resurrected children.
Note: the purple storm cloud
of the little downtrodden mouth?
But me—
still in the foster care of two pickled ovaries—
each day dig
coffins in air with fluttering
eyelashes,
        irony.

Thirty
hours of yesterday
have pinched my thighs varicose and hot
gravel on county roads, tar on city pavement
perfume the lost soles
of my feet, breasts

                              hang

from limp wrists—
            No—!
No more glad-handing with the übermensch!
I have seen God
smurfed by Evangelists tearfully
kissing their kneecaps on pay
television, while at clouds I merely:
                    Cough!

                    and they willie-wah across the sky
like drunks shooed by cops.

Hullo   Clumsy-footed angel,
Our hearts, lazy
as Jell-O,
glower in corners, spit
at potential lovers—

                                        ("What?What?What?What!
                                        Do you want from me!"
                                        "Nothing!Nothing!Nothing!"
                                        That's right,
                                        bald pated cupola,
                                        I am no bric-a-brac bride of Christ.)

Moon!
Hysterical! Mine!
My womb, virgin, Lady
of the Mountain
Lion, licking her whisker clots—
Oh, soul—
vagina, more
muscular than a vaulter's pole (sans teeth).
My legs are banisters to heaven,
my kneecaps God's
polished handholds:
He maketh me lie down in a May
bed of wet
moss,
trillium. Time!
You're as crude as a hangnail—
will you at least immortalize my French?

When a child asks—*What is the grass, Papa?*
Answer—*Petite ouverture, mon coeur.*
Between us
I am as lonely as the sixth bullet
in its so cold chamber,
mon frère.

O Merciful God (and Some Angels)

I stand at the kitchen counter sharing cookie crumbs with an ant—
one for me, one for you, no, please sir,
have two. Listen—
an angel overhead is brushing her lap after lunch—
wind licks the trees
like a rough cat bathing her kittens,
dirt *Stats* against the windows, curtains shiver on the rod, heave
sickness, Oh—
Death owns my house again, I crouch
to the World like a dog at the feet of an irascible master—
Please, Boss!

Centuries of grieving form a guerrilla army and obfuscate the landscape
with platitudes, prayers, and principles the consistency of rusks.
The Greatest Happiness defeats my army with an abacus.
Then Reason leg-irons love, quarantines compassion—
heaves all counterarguments in the river where they float
like alphabet soup. Still Death hopscotches
every syllogism crosseyed.
So I catapult my virtues, cloying and jittery like balls of mercury,
at angels, barter religious ecstasy to co-pilot the white bowl of souls across the
    violet water.
Finally desperation's centripetal force slings whole treatises
at the enemy in heaven—
justice is fairness,
not mercy,
pay up.

The pawpaw leaf tips backwards, then
gracefully tumbles
like a fisted hand opening
at death.
The inchworm holds the barren node, and
kisses it all over, kisses
it again,
like a sleeping face.

This Is Why

God's prayers for us are root vegetables
that struggle to breath and stretch
in clay.

Some grow into angels
with stolid bodies of
fennel and carrots, celery,

with lazy brains that fluster
in wind, get beaten down by rain,
matted in autumn muck.

These are not the angels with wings
the size of sequoia canopies
or robes soft as bumblebee fur, though some

are messengers,
onions, we unwrap silk by
sweating

silk, until
we find the little mooncalf we buried
that fall, for good,

now hiding in its monk's cell, wailing
with its wringing
hands. This is why

we weep
so much. More
than God

himself
I love
the earth angels

who taste like cold
dew, red
mud, my
fingers.

Moscow, 1999, the Women

Outside the university compound—
where five hundred international women scholars are meeting
on the subject of women and the environment—
in a public park—
an acre of dandelions, Lada tires, deadfall—
two middle-aged women in black raincoats sit hip-to-hip on a locust log,
one holding up a blue-sky umbrella under the despondent May rain,
the other reading out loud from a little book in the language of Akhmatova and
    Tsvetaeva,
her voice resonant as a porcelain bell over the brag-blare
traffic on Leonova Street.
Their warm jug of black tea,
butter cake in a yellow hat box.

At the subway entrance, Lenin's "museums of the people,"
grinning babushkas and their sallow daughters
and the sallow daughters of the sallow daughters
hold up swimming kittens and puppies by the neck scruff.
A green-eyed, yellow kitten arcs pee on a customer's open-toed shoes—screams,
laughter fall
into the subway hole, ricochet
against the marble walls and patriotic statuary.
The kitten,
sold,
no child's pet.
Evening, after it's done—
the mitten pelt pinned like a butterfly on the bathroom clothesline—
sweet Easter kulich,
black tea tasting like cedar smoke.

Betrayal

Moths fly inside the nimbus of lamplight by the bedside.
As larvae, they ate the faux silk pillowcase
my grandmother embroidered
with pomegranates and plums
just after we were married.
Shaved cedar won't deter them
nor drops of wormwood,
not even the broken mothballs
I sprinkle in the linen drawers.

I once held your first two fingers in my mouth
as you recited, slowly,
a recipe
for blackberry
blancmange. Your fingertips were coarse.
I tasted tobacco.
But I forgave you.

Shiners

I climb toward the headwaters of Mill Creek
and where the Appalachian Trail crosses the creekbed
squat down in the path of the midmorning sun,
so they can see me in my shadow,
so I can see them.

Because two-legs are supposed to keep walking in the direction of afternoon,
because something that's different is something gone wrong,
it takes a long time,
an almost graveside stillness
before they will come out from under the rocks.

Jesus bugs are oblivious.
Two one-armed crayfish sling silt at woozy moss.
I sit with my mind tucked under my wing like a sleepy heron

until the first shiner melts out of a silvery rock,

then more shiners
in a shallows so clear they seem to levitate just above the gold pea gravel,
shy as new silk.

When I sink my limp fist to the muddy bottom
shiners scatter-burst,
a darting scream, filmy chaos
in which I lose myself, again.

But after some time a shiner enters the hand-house I've built,
and the current in there contracts and expands and it feels as though I have hold
of the first pulse of Adam.

Then my own heart beats once less lonely,
ashes in my mouth taste less bitter,
and I remember how even his God had to rebuild covenants with life like this.

Wilson's Cows
Glass Hollow, Virginia, October

When Wilson calls his Guernseys: *Co-o-m-m-e—*
                        on,   C-o-o- m-m-e-

            on,
cows and half-suck calves
                    walk single-file
slow
        off the first red ridge
                 of the Blue Ridge,
down
        through the burnt-sugar smell
                of sassafras and maples,
           blackstrap
                burbled over feed
                     on freezing
                          February mornings.

When Wilson calls: *C-o-o-m-m-e-*
                      on. Come-
        on,
the lead cow
        with the white hood for a head
           canters
              across Mill Creek
        out onto the east field—
                stubbled up,
                  frost-bit brown, already—
then into the open pen,
where heaped-up piles of new hay look like green gumdrops.

As Wilson calls his stragglers
                he's hunched on his muddy four-wheeler,
           a scythe
                    with a blue cap on top, watching
his folded hands,
            like a loaf of brown bread in his lap,
the cripple little terrier beside him, rapt
                          as a cocked pistol.

When Wilson calls his one Charolais and her August calf:
      Co-o-m-m-e—on
Come—
        on—

  (They have stopped in the creek to wash the sweet-chalk of persimmons from their
    mouths)

wind

    fusks the willow—yellow fish flutter midair,
                          swimming
sun,
    and sweet gum leaves fall
              over the black backs in the pen
like a laying on of hands.

As Wilson calls *C-o-o-m-m-e-*
    on,
        the white calf kicks
                for nothing. She is
so happy
    following her mother through the late day

                        sun, the mother
            who will sit by the pen
                  for three days after
           the truck is gone,
                whose teats will whimper milk
                for weeks.

It's for this one
        I'll refuse loving
            the world
for a while,
    turn bitter
        remembering
the ashes
    and ashes and ashes and ashes
            the ashes
I've scattered over fields like this
and turn my back on the old man who, last June,
        called me,
           C-o-o-m-m-e-
   Come down from the road,

to give me a milk-pail of sour cherries
for jam.

Song, with Angus

The cat with his underbite looks like a bony old man
without teeth. Not
Grendel who tortures blind rodents and once
that rabbit, meek
as Christ.

When I curl the fine-toothed comb under his chin,
he rolls his blue eyes.
When I rake out his chops
he closes
his eyes.
As I comb out the top of his head,
whorled like a grey thumbprint,
he folds his hands in front of him,
then sets his heart down
on top of them
against his pink pads.

When I find a flea kicking in the comb
I mash it into
nothing,
then wonder—
Why have I done this?

Oh what do these two hands want?!

Some people wrap their hands together
like a closed tulip
on arm stems
and pray. Others
swing their arms like oars
on either side of a boat,
scudding over dark water.

Me,
I wring my hands until
they throb,
then pull them apart again.
Their sadness limned so fine
I can sing it
in a key
that's almost the key of
joy.

And for a while I am safe from myself.

I Loved the Black Cat

Who stayed in the woodshed with me
During sudden summer thunderstorms late at night.

I miss the man who stayed in our house
Afraid, but I think I did not love him

So much as I loved that cat.
Darkness came undone at seams of lightning.
Black cat sat. Still.

You know how wind leaps on top a bull pine's back, rides it nearly to the ground?

Well, cat just flared his leather nose a little,
Paws Buddha-tucked.
Watched on.

When thunder cracked its thirty knuckles, helved its three free fists, when rain spat
   sideways at us—

Cat snuffed—*Pfsss*—
So what?

Some storms were so sudden and spectacularly
Terrible, I'd run half-dressed to the woodshed from our house,

Where I'd find my black cat
Staring down my terrible,
When the man inside the house could not.

This Is about Darkness

The forsythia eats sunlight
near the open barn door
where Bill Perry stands in his overalls watching
his dappled-gray Percheron, Pike.

The largest horse on record was a Percheron,
a mare, twenty-one hands
high. This stallion stands, easy,
at nineteen.

Pike can pull a cadillac up Humpback Mountain
in a headwind.
He's made from endurance
like a hummingbird.

A torso poured from macadam, pressed
without interstices.
Hooves blue as wild violets growing along the roadside,
he jolts fenceposts when he trots.

Some sixth sense senses Bill.
Pike whinnies, rocks his huge head
No all the way to the dark
doorway. And the way

darkness takes him inside
that doorway
he might just as well be
a gnat.

The forsythia eats sunlight
near the open barn door
where Bill Perry stands,

the darkness,
watching.

Bitterroot Valley Nocturne

Late this afternoon Lasko's old white watchdog, neglected
for centuries, walked away from the sheep she'd been keeping.
While their muzzles were deep in hay drifts
she pressed her head against the barbed wire, as I whispered:
puppy, puppy, unmatting the frozen hair over her blue eyes,
so she could finally
close them.

And under my feet I felt the taut skin of the earth
go slack.

In early winter these brittle, brown foothills of the Sapphire Mountains
remind me of the little sleep scabs
I wanted to brush, gently, with my middle finger,
from a friend's eyelashes as he talked about how he'd follow his estranged wife
anywhere to hold his just nursed daughter at bedtime,
the weight of her like a sack of loose pearls.
For him she is the nearest neighbor's light I look for over at Laughing,
three miles east across these bluing late-day fields,
and in white-outs when the west wind throws whole horse pastures of snow
    overhead,
wishing it were young again.

At five it's nearly dark in the direction of the Sapphire Mountains.
Someone bends over our hemisphere to see that we're all right,
blocking the light,
who could it be?

Thinking of Kierkegaard

I've never told you that you talk in your sleep,
how I steal poetry from you
as you dream.
I never told you about the woman who calls each evening,
how strained her soft voice is,
that I'm writing a story
imagining your infidelity.

Your shoes are two dark holes
I would never step into,
though I might whisper into that abyss
now and then.
Trust is a very high trestle.

You walk it on a dare
in front of an audience,
and it's the idiot who does not tremble, even though
the sky is the most innocent blue,
and there is just wind, your hair, a bird calling into the gorge.

Song for Myself

Whenever my grandfather would say
"You are lonely," I'd think it
was yet another insult,
"She's so quiet,"
      "Too sensitive,"
            "Sad, sad, sad,"
or that I was supposed to do something about it
like the mark in fifth-grade math, or
that loneliness was something to hide in the secret compartments
        of jackets or wallets or in a deep
         pocket, deeper
than any human hand
      could reach,
in the darkness that's the darkness that's a
           hole,
and not a dead end,
or even my right eye's blindness.

Whenever my father said "You are
lonely," I would cry
      out, I would button
    the buttons at my collar
like Mary against
Gabriel when he said "Greetings,
      Favored One,"
when he said "God knows
    woman. God is
in your soul
the way the white thread is in the eye of your needle."

And she felt
the violation for only a moment for
after all
        He was He and wasn't He
entitled to walk through every room in His Kingdom
                and His word was the Word
"lonely." So
      I was
lonely,
       whatever that was.

Once when my husband said
I was lonely, we were walking
through the old coal town where
I was born, through its veils
of carbon and the damp-soot smell of immigrant miners
not too long in this country,
among men whose words cracked
           like eggs,
whose laughter was grease
           thrown in a hot skillet,
the same as their anger,
and the women's words to their children
were chewed
      for a long time,
then nibbled against their bluish mouths
           or directly into their ears
         like sprung
             question marks,

as my husband's voice castered across cement sidewalks reciting
                    the names of my streets
                              in my
                                   town, pointing

which way
              was the way
through my
town, and that was the first day
                                   I

went the other way.

And was lost
on a street where frame houses raised
their dresses into wide porches
and squat
              down
                        as women
once dropped newborns
without a sound onto the moss.

In the dark vestibule of a blue house
I saw a girl in a simple white smock
                              rolling a raw yolk
with a stick
              down a long hallway.
And when I asked her the name of her game
                              she told me
it was her secret.

So I followed her.

Scapegoat Mountain, Montana

The east sky's pink tongue laps up darkness.
A ripe moon lowers herself into an empty cedar snag,
My food bag hung there like a loose snood.
If the Rockies are the backbone of the world
Then surely Scapegoat is its vestigial tail.
I wake in Welcome Pass,
Dew-scales frozen all over the tent flap.

Always on the first day my mind lopes and sidles
Like a wild animal in dangerous country:
Not grizzlies or starvation, not snow squalls
Out of Alberta turning early August's green-
Gloss and blue-brusque
Into charcoal chiaroscuro
In only one hour. No.

I carry myself up the first nine mile grunt
Like a question mark, more like Atlas
Than Basho. At Straight Creek
When I take off my pack
I dizzy like a mote, afraid
To stand up to the wind, north wind
Realigning the tailbones of the eastern Front as far south as the Crazies.

On the third day I cross the Dearborn five times in the morning.
Each time that cold creek clasps my knees
Winnowing me. Once, I kneel down in the garbling water,
Mean to hold my mind just above it:
I'm knocked senseless,
The understanding's popped like a cork as I go
(Under. Up there sunskittering across the like-like-like-like-like I) lunge-

—Got it. Luscious
Yellow. Lupine warbling
Purple over on the mudbank.
Elk calf wafts water. My breath
A slow canter. O, let everything
Stand for itself as it is so

—

Something's rubbed the light so clear up Scapegoat massif
I can count cliff lice—wild nannies
And kids across the rock face—
From four thousand feet below. Halfmoon
Park's always in shadow, a bowl full of snow even in August,
Collecting skip-clap, asyntactical scree, quavery vowels, cracked
Consonants. Silence.

One week and I'm eight thousand feet up the massif.
From here wheat prairie and blue sky converge on a chink
At the receding eastern horizon.
From up here the Rockies protrude from the hide of this lean animal
Loping in three infinite directions.
Though this is not the afterlife,
Not quite.

Cloud-floaters above the crevasse. I squat inside the mountain drinking tea, eating
    oranges.
The little stove gasps for air, goes out.
A millennium's sediment compressed to a finger-width compressed
Between eight thousand feet of finger-widths.

Heat's quiet rasp-rasp at the rock,
Water and wind scatter generations in a single runnel and puff.
This old animal lopes slow.

The white belly of the east sky lifts up over the world.
Two great horned owls greet day
The old way. Song-soughs, purled prayers,
Clacking beaks. My flint lisps
Fire. Sunrise, warm
Bread and coffee. I walk out
Welcome.

In the dark little bar on the plains in Dupuyer
I eat white bread, butter and red onions, drink long-neck bottles of beer.
Two in the afternoon and old man Bryce behind the counter peels another one.
Says I smell worse than most who come out of there
"And them onions won't help it none," smiles,
Hums some Bob Wills tune.
I hoot the bottle.

Outside wind shoves the building one-millionth millimeter west a minute,
As Bryce tells those old stories:
Half-ton pickups take the wind-jammed roads in low gear,
Small kids wear weights around their ankles,
Dogs run in place.
Stars stammer overhead tonight as I lean way back through the east doorway.
"Let go that door frame, Lady." Bar roof yelps;
Wind holds me.

Ars Poetica

A cherry tomato on a white plate
language chases after
but can't skewer. Philosopher's headache.
Poet's itch.

All thoughts are words—necessary and sufficient
conditions for each other—
or nothing.
Such beautiful nonsense, the tomato taunts the fork.

Late yesterday I planted
the feedstore's mystery variety
with barely articulated leaves and
rambling main stem, threaded roots
knotted into a near perfect
cube. Stunted

from living too long
in the same dollop of dirt. Today
the tomato plant
relaxes into a new geometry:
down into the composting darkness,
up into the light.
Soon, a super-
numerary of yellow blossoms. Soon, little tomatoes
I chatter after with my fork.

But not nothing.

Case Histories for the 20th Century

> The wilderness has a mysterious tongue.
>
> —P.B. Shelley

A. *Emily D.*

Are you perfectly powerful?
(It was some months later that I was able to convince her she was talking English.)

Will you punish me?
(But she would never begin to talk until she had satisfied herself of my identity by carefully feeling my hands.)

Are you too deeply occupied to say if my Verse is alive?
(Alongside the development of the contractions there appeared the deep-going functional disorganization of her speech.)

What would you do with me if I came in white? Have you the little chest to put the living—in?
(She aptly described this procedure, speaking seriously, as a talking cure, jokingly as "chimney sweeping.")

I trust you received the flower the mail promised to take you. My foot being incompetent?
(The patient could not understand why dance music made her cough.)

Think you these thirsty blossoms will *now need naught but—dew?*
(She lived on only fruit, such as melons, etc., so as to loosen her tormenting thirst. She no longer conjugated verbs.)

Is immortality true?
(So long as I was talking to her she was always in contact with things and lively.)

I found a little bird this morning, down—down—on a little bush at the foot of the garden, and wherefore sing, I said, since *nobody hears?*
(As she came into the room, she had seen her pale face reflected in a mirror though it was not herself she saw, but her father with a death's head.)

Say, is he everywhere? Where shall I hide my things?
(Disagreeable events of this kind were avoided by my always [at her request] shutting
her eyes in the evening and giving her a suggestion that she would not be able to open
them until—)

Could you tell me how to grow—or is it conveyed—like Melody—
(—I did so myself the following morning.)

—Witchcraft?

B. *Sigmund F.*

Is it really the case that, apart from the sexual instincts, there are no instincts that do
not seek to restore an earlier state of things;
(I thought of his Forest and Sea as a far off Sherbet.)

that there are no instincts that aim at a state of things which has never been attained?
(Papa had still many Closets that Love had never ransacked.)

Must we follow the hint given us by the poet-philosopher, and venture upon the
hypothesis that living substance at the time of its coming to life was torn apart into
small particles,
(Mother was paralyzed Tuesday—a year from the evening Father died. I thought
perhaps he would care—)

which have ever since endeavored to reunite through sexual instincts?
(I knew a Bird that would sing as firm as the center of Dissolution.)

May we venture to recognize in these two directions taken by the vital processes the
activity of our two instinctual impulses: the life instincts,
(The Hens come to the door with Santa Claus—)

and the death instincts?
(—and the Pussies washed themselves in the open air without chilling their Tongues.)

And how shall we expect the mind to react to this invasion?
(He argued with the Birds—he leaned on Clover Walls and they fell, and dropped
him—with jargon sweeter than a Bell, he grappled Buttercups—)

Must this be so?
(—and they sank together, the Buttercups the heaviest.)

Are we afraid at bottom?
(Icebergs italicized the sea.)

Are we afraid at bottom of the emergence of this compulsion with its hint of
possession by some "daemonic" power?
(Today he asked me what "Genius" meant? I told him none had known—The
Grasshopper is a burden.)

After Metaphysics, or When the Fly Leaves the Flybottle

Just when I'm ready to call in the day and put it to bed without supper
you send the mockingbird who plays with his musical zipper,
exposing the World's underlife.
You send perfume from the autumn olive
whose septillion flowering ears are full of bees
singing songs for the revolution.
Out back Jake's Creek is speaking in tongues—
Missed you-missed you-missed you.

You wear me down, obsessively
rubbing your hands along my better judgment,
kissing the upturned noses of all my higher principles, until
my clothes are big as a mast sail,
until my longing leavens one thousand wedding cakes,
my longing is an undertow, and all the tourist beaches are posted: *Danger.*

Come for me—I'll break off my arms and will them to a body
of water, hang my legs up in overalls at night
so they won't come after us, feed
English to the birds in sweet pats of butter.

Then our loving gets raucous—
white moths yapping their wings—you wag, you
    wag in the little fingerbowl of me.

Your verbstem assumes declensions of mythic proportions.
My vowel sounds open on the south-most *hallelujah* side of the mountain.
Then metaphysically speaking we've stopped speaking
metaphorically—Silence

nuanced as a landscape in snow.

Snowflakes

Snowflakes are fools God sweeps out of his kitchen.
Last night he emptied his dustbin all over western Montana
and we sure got a load of them
on top of everything else.
No wonder snow falls in such a light-headed mizzy,
makes us all silly,
immune, we believe, to all life's unreasonable demands—
our own children
when they become strange to us,
parents when they are frighteningly familiar because we've become
them, lovers
who want us to be their parents and children.

I spent this morning watching the border collie on Highway 200
chasing magpies from a road-killed deer. Entitled,
so spit-snapping-angry
that by noon when a golden eagle blew down
(that pitbull of raptors, known to airlift live lambs)
the dog hadn't yet had her first mouthful.

Had it been me I would have run home hurting for sympathy
and bit off my good husband's right ear,
kicked my own scat at my frightened children,
sung the family dirge: *Injustice!*
Then spent days as a field post, alone,
arm-wrestling with the winterly west wind.

At dusk the dog came home with one anvil-shaped hoof in her mouth,
    seemed glad to have it.

Skiing Slough Creek, Yellowstone, February 9

Done a dumb thing,
trying to cross the drifted mile meadow down the middle,
break trail through a bowlful of sugar, butt-deep.

Now forward takes the exertion of a glacier,
turning back, a wish
blowing out candles at thirty-six.

And the white-out moving up the valley like the underwing of some deranged angel.

Do I take it standing?
Kneel?

A few yards south five cow bison
hunker under blue spruce in an acre basin.
Stretch my arms wide-out, whisper—*Sisters,
save me.*

Then God flips on all the celestial lights.

Meteor showers of wet kisses pelt my bowed head,
while huddled, hugger-mugger, wind wags all of me
like a scolding finger.
Until I love

every cat's paw cruelty, abandonment's ash
mask, my alum
kiss, my
unrequited lust, the begging
baby bird beak of enraged
loneliness,
the slap!—

the copperhead who bit
my bare
heel once. Love
the beating,
love it for its own sake,
then it stops.

Hip-deep,
            six bison
                        breaking trail
behind me.

December 10

—B.

Last night a single goose flew over the house,
throwing her voice out ahead of herself:
a stone
skipping out across still water.

A joy ride.

Then she followed the beautiful sound
across a meadow of moonlight and snow,
a clean bowl
waiting to be filled with the most delicious thing.

Camped Twenty Miles up the Teton River
outside the Bob Marshall Wilderness
on the Night Before a Wedding

The air begins, just, to smell like the deep bottom of a mossy well,
because good luck is moving southeast along the Rocky Mountain Front
into the wheat,
where four groomsmen, cocked
at three A.M., will squeeze
inside the Deere cab,
take the summer's second cut, as tumid
drops of rain clatch
the seedhead.

These four horses smell it coming from as far away as Heart Butte.
Restless, belled, they
Pong-dee-
Pong...
            Pong...
grazing the gravely flank of the river bed.

                              Clop!

Moon opens her brazen eye
on the white's tight rump—
a boulder
awash in muscle, swag, suppling,
feral as spring
melt.

Any woman with less sense would follow him all the way to the Ukraine
but me,
for my life has finally found a still place,
like the penny at the bottom of a deep well,
and I like it here.

Morning, the white, somebody's favorite, is saddled,
the others loaded with three weeks' backcountry gear,
led through sleeting rain up Wapiti Canyon.
Six miles.
Then the Bob.

Outside of Richmond, Virginia, Sunday

It's the kind of mid-January afternoon—
the sky as calm as an empty bed,
fields indulgent,
black Angus finally sitting down to chew--
that makes a girl ride her bike up and down the same muddy track of road
between the gray barn and the state highway
all afternoon, the black mutt
with the white patch like a slap on his rump
loping after the rear tire, so happy.
Right after Sunday dinner
until she can see the headlights out on the dark highway,
she rides as though she has an understanding with the track she's opened up in
   the road,
with the two wheels that slide and stutter in the red mud
but don't run off from under her,
with the dog who knows to stay out of the way but to stay.
And even after the winter cold draws tears,
makes her nose run,
even after both sleeves are used up,
she thinks a life couldn't be any better than this.
And hers won't be,
and it will be very good.

Pastoral

Let the roadside go to chicory
and gall-
of-the-earth, and the hillside go
to clover
and everlasting
pea, and the road itself
to the barred belly of the blacksnake
and the tarot belly
of the tortoise,
while burdock and poke
choke the corn
out of the fields,
and morning glories run wild
over the immaculate gardens—
let thistle grow tall
and defiantly purple.
And let there be no noise,
just the pileated woodpecker
screeching
like a wild monkey,
heat,
and the wind stumbling through a long row of pines,
the unabashed turning
of leaves
asking
the wind's *blessings, blessings, blessings.*

Spirit Walks Through Miasmic Melt and Mud,

mid-flank in muck. Eleven geese fly overhead:
eleven coccyxes of a species flying into extinction;
the eleven knees and elbows of love under the bedsheets;
eleven fingers' pressure on the womb.
God flies the other way, drags
the catch rope.

Dissonate Psalm in Late Summer

Their music goes out through all the earth, Their words reach to the end of the world.
    Psalm 19

At eight o'clock I eat the letters *O*
and whorled bananas
floating in a puddle of warmed milk.
At three I dream the dream
of my mother's missing breast—
the blood orange laid open, outraged.
Five o'clock
I walk out, watch the robin kicking at the mud,
his slack worm,
his convulsive gold eye
strafing the ground.
Behind me the cat's red bowl coughs
across the white linoleum. She's hungry too.
The robin flies. The worm...
Each day ends

the same. Suppertime,
I take my own bowl to the backdoor.
Dark mask over the world,
moon in the mouth-hole.
Satellite's red ellipses.
A firefly blips on the door screen. Prodigious.
Drawling
mosquito blesses the blood. Frog
groans for the dragonfly—

Little psalmist, the wild lake in your throat is thrumming!
Midnight,
wind blows east against the larch and even the larch lets go a gasp of yellow
needles. (Oh—
why
is the human heart so cinctured?)

Today, all day, the World's skirl in the silence,
so clear.

Notes

The epigram is from Rilke's "Book of Monastic Life" in *The Book of Hours,* translated by Anita Barrows and Joanna Macy, Riverhead Books, 1996.

"Geronimo, Running" is from an exercise with the *I Ching*. I have borrowed and altered a few lines from that text.

"A Few Words about Myself, My Dear Mayakovsky": Marina Tsvetaeva uses the term "clumsy-footed angel" in "To Mayakovsky."

Sources for "Case Histories for the 20th Century": Emily Dickinson's letters; Josef Breuer's "Anna O," from *Studies on Hysteria* published jointly with Freud; and Freud's *Beyond the Pleasure Principle*. I've taken minor liberties with a few pronouns, verb tenses, and phrasings.